BRINK

First published in 2025 by
The Dedalus Press
13 Moyclare Road
Baldoyle
Dublin D13 K1C2
Ireland

www.dedaluspress.com

ISBN 9781915629487 (hardback)
ISBN 9781915629494 (paperback)

Dedalus Press titles are available in Ireland
from Argosy Books (www.argosybooks.ie) and in the UK
from Inpress Books (www.inpressbooks.co.uk).

Cover artwork 'Enclosure on a Mountain'
by Maria Simonds-Gooding, by kind permission.

Dedalus Press receives financial assistance from
The Arts Council / An Chomhairle Ealaíon.

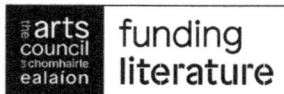

the arts council
chomhairle ealaíon | funding literature

BRINK

CIAN FERRITER

DEDALUS PRESS

Contents

⌒

to Deirdre, Luan and Síofra
the measure of my dreams

Brink

Between shifts, the nurses off-guard,
you climb into bed beside me,
tenderly re-arranging lines and tubes
until you can wrap your arms
around my wilted torso –

the arms that wrapped around me
against a Leitrim snowdrift high as a house,
under a swollen Saharan moon,
up a laneway off Liffey Street
as we tumbled back from a gig,

under the black canopy of an oak
on Old Head, the Atlantic whistling,
on the mossy floor of a Wicklow wood –
the arms that have held our lives to account,
that carry me, now, back from the brink.

Snowball

I have fallen out of the world
this February night and landed here
at the marsh's edge, reeds about me
like the masts of listing galleons.

I can go no further. A newt
flexes his crested spine like the dragon
on the silk gown of the Emperor Zhu Di –
he of Perpetual Happiness –

as the Emperor watches what remains of his fleet
limp into the swollen mouth of the Yangtze,
mist rising, his eunuch entourage
readying for retreat to the hills.
His departure, later, marked by a single
gong of the North Temple's bell,
horse hooves disappearing into the wood,
the moon a snowball breaking on a black roof

and landing now six hundred years on
as droplets on my brow,
my pallor the Emperor's pallor
as he starts at a rustle in the undergrowth

and contemplates for the first time
the terror of death.

Ghost Ship

I have seen your house adrift in the strangest
of places: in Cassidy's top field, smoke
spilling from the chimney. In a clearing
in Hartigan's Wood, wet shirts hanging
between two pines. Against the stump of the keep

beyond Moran's, the crooked gable-end
taking rain; and, one night, jutting out
over the lip of the quarry, a light on
in the kitchen, the whole place teetering.

This morning, in thinning mist, it is back
where you last left from it. Lace curtains
neatly parted, lavender turning to spit,
crab-apples pocking the grass. The gate-latch
rattling like a freshly turned prayer wheel.

The Day the Satellites Went Down

His car engine was still running,
miles from where they found him.
A trail of sorts in his wake –

muddied shoe, phone glinting
like a dropped earring, jacket suspended
from a branch like a small life.

No one could work out why
he chose this spot. *Never more alive,*
he said, later. Crown of his head

pressed through the gap, fern fronds
like jump leads against his temples,
his tongue lapping the black juice of the bog.

Still talked about in the office.
From the desk that used to be his,
I replay the scene: low gasps, light breeze,

the soft pink soles of his feet
quivering, like a new-born
filling his lungs with alien air.

Hem

Evenings when
you were not yet back
I'd sit on the makeshift
bench in the yard

of our first house
where you'd hung
a line with room
for just one dress

close my eyes
and wait for the breeze
to lift your hem
against my knees.

Limbo

The ward reduces to its midnight hush.
A week since you were born six weeks too soon,

we keep vigil in this touchless limbo.
Your face a miniature in distance,

your fingers gripping invisible lines.
Deirdre expressing to your silent cries.

In the small hours, without a word, a nurse
releases you into your mother's arms.

Sensing your breath in that titanic hold,
I wrap my shaking self around you both.

Republic

The River

The eddies, where she entered, scattered like eels,
her mother's fur coat in the downdraft
was a raft of otters turning for the deep.
The No. 9 bus on the bridge above crossed
from north to south, its driver nearing shift's end.

Her ripples were no bigger than a carp's,
her weight displaced in the dark flow,
the same weight I see in her daughter,
and in her daughter's daughter,
when we cast through midge clouds in evening heat.

The Search

There were things the old hands took as signs,
starting the search at Lady's Island:
a curlew's nest empty in July –
a sword handle staking the mud at low tide,
its jade dragon spitting fire –
engraved, above the initials MMcE,
'Korea '50 to '53'.

They found her hat on an alder branch,
hanging the way it hung in the hall.

The Funeral

The cortège stretched a good half-mile,
a slow tributary sliding into the cemetery's basin.

No headstone yet over her husband's grave,
although the anniversary had long passed.

She couldn't bring herself to visit, it was said.
Flowers withered there like weeds sprayed in a ditch.

They came from as far as Derry,
her people in the main.
Men sweating in suits,
women touching mantillas.

Some of the talk was angry, all of it was low –
how does a mother do that to her own?

My Mother

I wheel my mother along the shore path,
because she's always loved the water.
Her hair blow-dried, white, shining in the sun,
pipits flitting and skipping in the shallows.

I recall the day on Silver Strand when she bolted,
naked, into the Atlantic, and we followed
her lead, roaring at the big sky,

our togs strung out along the sand
as if a clothesline had been yanked
from its posts and thrown over the shoulder
of a mother proclaiming her own Republic.

The Sea

She points to where to stop. We stop.
She folds her hands, her eyes closing in the warm breeze.
My hands rest on her sparrow shoulders,

our pulses merging,
the sea taking all the river has to give.

Begley's Well

i.m. Séamus Begley, West Kerry traditional musician
(26 August 1949 – 9 January 2023)

I

Nearly half the stories were true.

His set in Baile na bPoc after the Battle
of Fionn Trá, blood flecking the buttons and bellows,
Kerry Blues bawling in the cliff field.
The night he raised Halla na Feothanaí
above Brandon with his mother's soft hands
as he squeezed life itself into air. Boots slapping
the dancefloor, dust and sweat spilling
before *Port na bPúcaí* lowered them to earth.
The evening Queen Victoria passed on donkey and cart,
the creature hoofing to a polka as her Highness
slid forgotten into Brandon Creek.

II

When for the last time he set his accordion down,
the sun beyond Binn Diarmada sank to its knees,
its bent head flooding the world's end. The wind,
mid-gale, stopped beyond Inis Tuaisceart,
cormorants and gannets froze mid-plunge.
In a pocket of astonished silence,
he stood with his arms outstretched and poured
the great jug of himself back into the well.

Fencing

Soft in the head (and harsher words again)
would greet your arrival into Dargan's,
you, sporting your electric blue headphones,

grinning as you played pool against yourself,
nursing your single pint of Rock Shandy
before you tractored back to the farm.

But you knew when a calf was too low
in the belly or scour by a heifer's gait,
the order that lay beneath the chaos.

The day I came to help with the fencing,
you beckoned me into the shed where
a line of CDs hung from a rafter by twine,

their silver teeth bared to frighten crows
and now, a foal who'd broken from his pen
and froze, fetlock in mid-air, as the sun

through the rafters flashed from Elton John
to Judas Priest to Dylan's *Tangled Up in Blue* –
small hooves falling to earth on brilliant hay.

Atlas Stone

The graveyard is the only ordered place
in this sweep of tossed rock and bog –
you would smile at that.

The wind is too warm
and from the wrong direction,
a sirocco thrown off course –
you'd smile at that, too.

The piper starts a low lament
and I hear the muezzin call
down that Atlas valley

where you sang *sean-nós* with the Berbers
and we developed the *Unified Theory
of Sadness and the Stone Wall,*
promising to test it on the five continents.

That was before your news.
Still time enough, you said,
to finish the wall by the stream.

I kissed some new-placed stones
so that the wind, when it blew,
would blow kisses back to you.
In the end, I finished it alone.

Ark

Rain – jungle rain, Niagaran rain, end-of-days rain –
hammering the roof and you not home, 2 a.m.,
your mother worrying – *still no sign of him* –
and me in bed beside her, smiling at the thought
of you freewheeling past the Met Office – rain shooting off
its cupped satellite dishes – down Washerwoman's Hill,
no hands, your wheels throwing up water-ski arcs of spray,
speeding up as you near the bridge, your spokes spinning
like turbines, your glowing face lifted to the deluge,
your hair streaming like a comet's tail as you take to the air,
clear the bulwark and land, sliding, on the deck of the Ark,
giraffes and ocelots scattering, the scent
of cedar unloosed where you stop, feet from Noah
who shakes his head from under a yellow sou'wester
as he turns the prow for Drumcondra, and beyond, for Ararat,
the sky brightening to the east as you leap into the garden,
the rain easing, your mother slipping into the deepest of sleeps.

Tarzan in the Phoenix Park

In 1924, Johnny Weissmuller swam in the pond in Phoenix Park Zoo as a contestant in the Tailteann Games which took place just after the Paris Olympics, where he had competed as a swimmer on the US team.

Today, the zoo's pond is jungle green, snake green,
alligator green, dangling vine-rope green,
steam and hiss and deadly piranha green,
Saturday picture house black-and-white green.

Chimpanzees swing through the park's canopy
of beech and lark, elephant trunks swish
in the mosquito shade of the magazine fort,
warthogs tussle near the Strawberry Beds.

Halfway down the course, Tarzan comes up
for air and from the crowd a man from Meath
starts the call that sounds as far as Tara,

while upstairs in a Chapelizod two-bed,
my granddad fixes his loincloth
and my granny mouths into the mirror: *Me Jane.*

Smeared

Bending to study the fallen frame
of a Red Admiral, I see lava flow
in angry rivers through cracked earth,

ice caps adrift in a hostile sea,
yanked antennae relaying no voices.
Dead flies litter her orbit like crashed ships.

The words of the old book come whispering:
ride with indifference this beauty, this terror.

Under touch she crumbles into dust,
leaving my thumb trembling and smeared
with what once lit up the orchard's leaves.

Last Rites

Uncle Jack once gripped a man's half-severed hands
while giving him last rites in Santiago.
Bullets puffing dirt from broken ground,
clothes strung above them in the narrow street
like echoes of the dead or missing.

At last, he gave up speech, sought answers
in what leaked through night-time's cracks,
bare bulb flickering in his top-floor flat.
Dawn light catching the sides of ashtrays,
cats tip-toeing between bottles.

A man who put others before himself
who fell holding out his hands to rain,
to his shadow opening large to meet him,
to love on the other side, waiting,
to clay returning, without interest, to clay.

Team Photo

Hindu Kush, Afghanistan, 1995

After the Taliban,
under a barrel in the village square,
six amputated hands.

I played football there once.
Posed, afterwards, thumbs up.
Peace upon us as our jeep moved on.

I find the picture, curled in an attic box,
study its jury of faces one by one:
shy, wary, ebullient.

Who now dresses with one arm?
Who held whom in place
as the blade came down?

The Sickbed of Shane

I

You spiked it, swilled it, slammed it, horsed it down,
bare-backed the feral wolfhound through the throng
of London's moshing, mongrel exiles,
lost soldiers looking for a soldier's song.

You plucked a feather from the pigeon's nape
and with it blew the sluice-gates open:
out they tumbled – roaring, fighting, spilling –
the punks who played melodeon in the barns

then smashed their heads against old England's walls
or bent the bow until the fiddle burned
or passed out cold under a petrol sky
in which you floated with your ancient grin.

II

You screamed the scream of silent labouring men
whose faces at last orders were curlews
fleeing gunshot, bog holes in a storm.
You saw in broken glass the heavens'

tender constellations: the hunter
laying down his gun; the ploughman sharing bread,
the bear refusing to be judged or judge.
And now, as you lie on your sickbed,

we've come to take your hand, to do what you
have done – to weigh in love the loser's lot,
to bend in to the man without a voice,
to whisper: *you are held, held and understood.*

Rescuing from Air

1. *Breanndán Ó Beaglaoich, accordionist*

Head tilted left,
he holds,

like a dying lover,
his accordion –

a row of tumblers
slides off a shelf.

2. *Eoin Duignan, uilleann piper*

In the pale Protestant light
of the Church of St James

his pipes in shadow
are curlews and corncrakes.

3. *Kane's, an hour before Pauline Scanlon sings*

A wet afternoon.
Goose prints across the floor.
Pints settling.
An opening door.

4. *Port na bPúcaí*

A caravan step, West Kerry, mid-Winter

Billy plays a slow
air on bouzouki

while the moon
picks out a hare's tracks
in the snow

which stops behind
a cylinder of gas

where steam
in hare's breath
rises.

5. *Con Durham, uilleann piper, takes a break*

Legs crossed
on the bench outside Bric's,
Con Durham
licks the skin of a rollie –

his eyes, in the half-light,
fixed on the ditch
for the fairy that might
make off with his chanter.

Me and Pangur Rua

for my dog, Charlie

I

Unemployed, at peace,
the couch
our cell and patch of grass.

II

Our plates –
clean-scraped, licked –
rest on smooth stone.

III

Our bellies
rise and fall
like kingdoms.

IV

Half-thoughts
cartwheel
through the silence.

V

You snarl
in your sleep.
Brave Setanta!

VI

A poem will soon arrive.
Bold scut –
don't even think of a chase.

Castle Avenue

Her house, though small, had rooms
we did not have at home:
the pantry, the scullery,
the good room – always locked.

Her back to us, mostly:
poking the grate,
stirring a pot,
pulling her cardigan close,

woollen skirt running down
to moleskin boots,
glimpses of veiny calf
like cathedral marble.

The four of us children slept
in the hollow of the bed
in the spare room,
like oversized mice.

Next to us on the landing: her room.
I ran into it once, for a dare:
dark wardrobe, window netting,
dust motes fuzzing the air,

the shock of her there –
wrinkled hand stubbing a saucer,
smoke streaming from her nostrils.
A life in her stare.

Curfew

Always, these days – the noise.
Her polytunnel shudders
as military trucks pass.

Her head behind plastic
might be a plant
gone to seed.

She tips the watering can over
tight green tomatoes. Drops
recoil before sliding into soil.

Peapods lie scattered
on a bank of manure
like spent shells.

Last week, her neighbour
found dead in his barn,
his broken windows still unfixed.

Tonight, after curfew,
she will leave food out for his dog,
wait all night for the hammering on the door,

reading poems,
old letters, history,
the *Tibetan Book of the Dead*.

Circles

On the death of an elderly monk in Thikse Monastery, Ladakh

In the monastery's wooden skip,
a wasp is whirring furiously
around the inside of an empty bottle
like a leathered motorcyclist
rimming the Wheel of Death.

Tiredness getting the better of him,
his circles start to flag until he comes
too close to the measure left for luck
by the mourning monks.
In the stillness after his final twitch,

he floats on the liquid's surface,
his wings beneath him like a shroud,
the antennae of his legs
transmitting him to his next life
through the dishes of my widened eyes.

True or Bluff

You told me once that a locket you found
in a flea market in San Francisco
was inscribed *J.C. 4.33*
and contained air from the studio
where John Cage's famous slice of silence

was first recorded, the silence being
the silence that followed the collapse
of the American Dream, the locket
pawned for hard drugs, its pocket of silence
long since filled with the dirty noise of life.

I told you in return that I met Cage once
at the end of a pier in West Kerry
where he was staring at two jellyfish
mating just beyond a bank of seaweed.

You pointed out that jellyfish don't mate
which, I countered, was exactly what Cage thought
before he turned and receded down the pier
into the black frame of Mount Brandon.

It is only now I realise that good
stories contain their own realities,
that bluff is the coward's way out when truth
loses her nerve or has no bed to anchor in.

You've gone. I spend my days bluffing badly
about a return that no myth can summon.

Three Snuff Bottles of the Ming Dynasty

I

You do not tell of the plum-dark night
Oxtail, the indentured boy, stole
across his master's floor to press
your jade face to his lips –

cinnamon and sloe,
bamboo and broken stone –
dreaming of the daughter
of the house, her soft mouth.

II

The bondsman knew before the last card
turned – Joker, manic-faced, juggling
long knives – that all was lost.
The bottle (emperor of a thousand broken

dreams) swallowed in the blood-silk
of a rival's pocket. Whinnying outside,
day about to break over the black
mountain known as Dragon's Lair.

III

A fake, so fine it was more precious
than the original. Rings
a little thick on the finger;
maple leaves curling away from,

not towards, the east.
When does a trained eye trump
the heart? There is an art
in surviving against all odds.

from Glasnevin Haiku

Great Palm House at night
monkey-screeches in the high trees
silent by morning

mist on the Tolka
what's next to break through –
swan? Viking canoe?

Dorset Street lock
Behan and a new friend
drinking in silence

behind the coal scuttle
a black cat
licks herself clean

bee stumbles out of the shed
missing, presumed dead –
October sunshine

this boy
on his father's shoulders
can see the whole world

Skimming stone –
the lives I could have led!
Circles rippling still.

ICU Bedwash

As if all the soft sponges of the sea
brushed over me, took hold of my skin,
dowsed the fire of my poisoned blood,

built a bridge over the slicked river of me
to where my garden used to be, water
dripping from curled leaves onto petals,

heads unbending as the greyness shakes free.
Wash my face, my chest, my shrinking legs,
renew my subscription to what it is

to be. Pull me to your chest. Hold me.

A woman sings in a flat
on Paradies Strasse, Munich

By a process of elimination,
I worked out that it was the grandmother
all along, her shoes one morning
the only pair left outside the flat next to mine,
voice lilting down the corridor
as if through a Mesopotamian valley:
women bent in fields straightening to listen
oxen lifting their heavy heads to stare,
swords blunting in the shade of fig trees,
an old farmhand sinking to his knees,
his sundered heart re-stitching note by note,
her door softly opening to where
I stand weeping, her eyes meeting mine,
the whole of history swirling in her gaze.

Night of the Big Wind, Glendalough, 1839

*"At one o'clock a most tremendous hurricane commenced which
rocked the house beneath as if it were a ship! Awfully sublime!
But I was much in dread that the roof would be blown off..."*
— John O'Donovan, *Ordnance Survey of Ireland,*
Glendalough, Wicklow, 1839

I swear I saw the round tower bend
like a sapling, the house rocking beneath us
a ship rounding the Magellan Strait,
the great bell swaying fiercely like a beast
trying to break its loud chains. Such giddy
terror! I knelt and prayed to our maker,
much in dread, that the roof not be taken
and tossed like spindle wood into the lake
whose angry spittle covered the fields.
Whether or not I was heard, or he answered,
dawn broke to birds flitting between fallen
branches, a calmness as if after battle.
The enemy vanquished but the heart –
like love – still brittle, quivering in its lair.

Keeper

Sure I'd best do it myself –
the words from your silhouette
at the front door at Crewbawn,
morning light settling around you,
the Boyne beyond, bending the earth.

By the time I follow you out,
arms puckered with stings,
you are high up the alder tree,
head lost in a swarm of bees,
like a man leaning in through a hatch.

Thunderclap as your box slaps shut,
you receding into the yard.

Later, your dusty red Datsun
pushing off down the avenue,
bees flooding the back window
like coins pouring into a hold.

The Little People

i.m. Tony McMahon

When he fixed me with a look and asked
if I understood that the little people
still moved among us, although harder
for them now with all the noise and concrete,
that he had seen two of them recently
emerge from a crack in the ground just there –
pointing to a ditch beside a garage
that housed forklift trucks and JCBs –
he wasn't looking for an answer
and I understood then for the first time
that when he closed his eyes on the back squeeze
of the box handed down from Joe Cooley,
he was where that ditch began
and not where the rest of us thought it ended.

Tauromachy

Tauromachy, it's called, this sculpture.
A bull's severed head, bronze, wedged
into the earth inches from its master's feet.
An abstracted pot-bellied farmer

with rod legs and a staff for a head,
he is steering his invisible herd along
an ancient track, dogs busy at the rear,
silent amidst the bellowing.

I look over to where you are leaning into
the line of a Giacometti and think to tell you,
later, how I'm back to the first time I met
your father. Watching him *hoosh* the last

of the cattle through a gap in a ditch
as we approached. How he sucked the pith
from a cigarette as he sized me up.
The tossed butt sizzling in a puddle.

The way you squeezed my hand and said
you're in as he receded into the hollow
of the top field like a matador
departing, undefeated, from the ring.

47

My Mother Returns to Boarding School

She hangs back, as the renovators let us in
to the place that became her home
when her mother was taken from her.

We set off across paint-spattered sheets,
the chapel's sullen windows
throwing blunt colour onto tile,

through the refectory, air thick
with buried smell, past her classroom's
closed door, to here – at the end

of a speckled corridor – the hall.
Her shoulders soften as she pushes up
the steps to the stage where she

once found, in applause, a proxy
for love. I try to coax from her a few lines
of a soliloquy, an encore

but she's stopped dead-centre, her eyes
a swoop of jackdaws re-entering a copse,
sixty years of ghosts still pulling –

through the silence, through the wan light,
through her tremoring fingers –
the ropes of the thick black curtain.

Irregular

Lispole, Kerry, Civil War, 1922

This track they've walked
a thousand times before

through whitethorn fuzz
and knee-high meadow grass.

Now Brosnan's hands are tied
with wire and Sheehy's gun is real.

They end up at the clearing
where Brosnan makes to run –

sunlight clots on leaves
below the scattering rooks.

Sheehy kneeling, spewing
by Brosnan's upturned boots.

Last Tour

Hardware store, Missouri, mid-July

The Discount for Vets sign brings him in,
his house badly in need of fixing.

Stars and stripes limp on high poles in the lot.
Rounding the aisle, paint-pots crash –

and he's back, Baghdad, the old bazaar,
head swivelling, fingers curled, roars

from behind, the dry, red dirt ablaze.
The flattening, scorching chopper blades.

His trolley rolling slowly to a halt
where silver hammers hang

in gleaming rows. His sobs.
The shop till's momentary pause.

Matsumoto

A wrong turn looking for a ruin
has me knocking on this open door.
She appears as if expecting me,
secateurs in hand – *the kettle's on, come in.*

Between the range and the photo
on the sill, delicate prints of birds
in flight lead to talk of Japan,
her decade in the East.

In the sunlit lean-to, she demonstrates
how to prune a bonsai oak:
tiny leaves falling, its acorns slipping
through cracks in the universe.

This tree grown from a cutting brought back
from Matsumoto. On a shelf above,
the glazed blue pot that travelled with them:
the ashes of the one she loved.

The Others

It was our scary film phase –
Friday nights in the living room,
biscuits, milky tea –
before I drifted out into adulthood.

I remember the start you got –
nail-marks on my arm, *Jesus Christ!* –
at the end of that scene
where a young girl is playing alone

in a room in a Gothic mansion,
singing to herself, back to the viewer,
and then turns suddenly, her face
an 80-year-old's, long dead.

When I came to visit recently,
I was the one to start when you turned
with a child's mild devastation
before returning wordlessly to the screen,

your white hair sticking out
over the top of the armchair
like a stand-in dummy
among discarded props.

Ballyvoheen Recital

Into the mattress of a neighbour's field,
at whose edge I stand sheltering from rain,
a piano – I swear – has fallen from a passing plane.

Its lid is splintered in a hawthorn ditch.
Its legs stand buried in puddled muck.
Its body lies still as an empty trough.

Six cows gather around it like druids
at gloaming on the equinox. One moves
forward, swishing her baton of tail,
bends to its bony shelf her hooded head –

joined by another, they soon work up a scale.
The chorus bellows out its ancient moans.
A force shoots up my spine and out my throat:
birth-howl, life-shriek, wind-rinsed note.

Tractor Rally, December Sunday

Ventry, Co. Kerry

Chariot after chariot they came
out of the un-Roman mist, adorned
with flags, bunting, blinking lights.
Reins held slack, elbows propped
on side-doors, fingernails tanged
with afterbirth, sons leaning
into them in flushed likeness.

Bringing up the rear, in orange hi-vis:
their Emperor. Cabinless, wheels
slicking bitumen, arcing spray, arms
sun-burnished, poised. His crown
a bank of bog cotton in a May gust.
Rolling southwards to an easy welcome –
chimney-smoke, window-light, dozing dogs.

Kung Fu Buffet

I have eaten all I can eat from
The All You Can Eat Kung Fu Buffet.
3 a.m. and no sleep since Tuesday.

My mother is everywhere – the outline
of her mouth in folds of fried rice,
her frown traced between left-over ribs.

The ladles protruding from the buffet
are listing cranes, falling swords,
my mother's arms at the post-mortem.

Bruce Lee in outsized profile faces me down
from the far wall, his chop-kick hurtling
in my direction. I will his assault –

collapse me, please, with one coiled foot.
Have my slumped body pulled off-screen,
an unnamed extra, and let me lie

in the bowels of the land of make-believe,
where I can hold her hands, nod, say nothing,
eat all I can eat of love.

Haunted

Sinéad O'Connor (1966–2023)

You beat from life's botched metal a coracle of gold –
numinous, thin-leafed, unsteady – that you'd row out
at midnight to the centre, where you waited for the air
to settle, for the raven to brush your slender throat.

You'd drag a chord up from the deep, dripping with the world's
old hurt, and swing it in our faces. Sometimes, you woke
shivering on the peat-black shore, reeds clenched in your fists.

You sang us through your terror and beyond, held the note
which ripped the locked doors open, dropped us at the dark pool
of our shame. When you fell, and fell again, a child slipping
from her mother's grip, we never reached to break your fall.

This morning, the sky broke bruised and heavy, light too tired
to show its face, lava buried under stillest ash.
People stopping where the grass gave out. The city silent.

Let us mark your resting place. No monument
to glory or to pain. No soaring spire, no pyramid
or spiralled tomb: just a woven mat, some beads, a bowl
and a candle flaming until kingdom come.

Car

I am eleven, at home and asleep.
Dreams spill over the ledge of silence.

The phone rings, tearing night out of shape.
I gravitate to the landing and watch,

through banisters, my father crumple
on the stairs in swabs of thin light.

I still hear his car splutter, pull away
up the hill, out the chough-black road,

on through the empty midlands,
to his mother stiff in a messy bed.

The days that follow. The mush of voices,
heat and curled-up sandwiches.

His chapped hands. The bowed heads. That shiny box.
His look as she is lowered into ground.

Garden Fence

A slat missing from the garden fence
sets me thinking of Walter Mann
who emerged from a bedroom
into our student lives

on a Munich Tuesday morning –
one leg shorter than the other,
his right hand missing a finger
clean from the knuckle.

The more of our beer he downed,
the wilder the tales:
Tuesday night, rolling a smoke:
Lost it in a card game in Belarus.

Wednesday evening: *Caracas –*
caught in bed with a butcher's wife.
Thursday morning, shaking his head:
A cobra in Bangalore, and then

Four women I fucked that night –
a bloodshot eye in the gap between
three raised and yellowed fingers,
his audience now reduced to one.

I saw him last that afternoon –
limping across the wet concourse,
clutching his windcheater tight,
receding step by listing step

like a drunk in search of the lifeboat
on a sinking ship.

Summer Clearance

Rijeka, Northern Croatia, 1993

Is that him on the TV report?
The pale one smoking –
or the one being covered up?

The young man in military fatigues
I saw last Summer, smoothing
his hair in the reflection

of a shop window, face white
despite sun, a barber's nick on his neck,
mannequins staring through him.

Who disappeared into a truck,
axles dripping as it pulled out
to head for an empty highway,

its radio crackling
a staccato of names:
Dubrovnik, Mostar, Srebrenica.

Patch

The vegetable patch
laid waste, again, last night
by a band of guerrilla slugs.

They spend their days rolling
cigarettes, fixing their bandanas,
snoring under briars.

But their time has come.
I have tipped the last of the home brew
into a battalion of spent tea-lights

and I lie in wait in the long grass.

Planting

Dead leaves like spirits lift, fly past
the handle of the spade, the trowel, the fence;
incant the heart's pent chaos.

Your fingers deep in worm and clay,
your raincoat, yellow, a private flare
sent up to mark where the world is made:
tight, small fists of life, still sleeping,

laid gently down, tucked into earth,
from where with time they'll burst –
your lips, your neck, your private smile.

Coal

She was a convent wall scaled,
smoke rings rising from behind
the parish hall, a ride hitched
on a fire tender. Her father's favourite.

She was fireflies bouncing against
an upstairs window. A fare-dodger
on the Isle of Man ferry.
No parent left by thirteen.

She raised six children. Never
fixed on the past. Ran marathons
in a red vest. A teacher who picked flowers
with the students who hated books.

In the end, an insomniac falling
asleep on the couch to Tom and Jerry.
The slow clap of a punctured wheel.

Her eyes, when she turned,
were two coal-bags of grief
pouring into a basement cellar.

View from a Shanghai Train

Thirty years of marriage
spent between three rooms.

On Saturdays she hangs
his work trousers

on the rooftop line
and beats them with a stick:

dust from his other woman's floor
rising like smoke from a wet fire.

Hanging On

Earl's Court, London, 1990

The sallow man with the wart on his cheek
is smoking outside the front door of his corner shop
under a faded sign
bearing someone else's name
and the words *Grocer* and *Tobacconist*
just about hanging on
like before him the rubber stamp man
the radio repairman
the ecclesiastical sculptor
the blue video man
the mobile librarian
the sewing machine salesman
the woman in the post office who sorted notes
with a red rubber thimble on her thumb
and especially
the boy with the green eyes
who fixed lawn mowers
and could whistle 'God Save the Queen'
through a blade of grass
picked from the cracks in the forecourt.

Letting Go

It is said in the annals that,
when a great master passes,
the sky over the mountains

flares up like the northern lights,
flesh and bone dissolving
as he becomes a rainbow body.

This morning the sky over Cabra
broke orange and crushed pink,
the windows of the 122 aflame

as it passed the seventeen shops.
Tony the postman found in his bed.
A murmuration of starlings

burst from the roof of St Peter's,
cars pulled over to let the ambulance pass,
tarmac slick as a raven,

the weathervane on his gable end
spinning like a Tibetan prayer wheel
as a mile above Phibsboro he entered

the bardo before the next realm.

World's End

Taking the sky road in the gloaming
when a leveret appears, the burnt Y
of her mouth frozen in this dark strait
between two continents of gorse,

my ship of war bearing down on her.
I veer left – and she leaps right.
What I hear as the engine cuts:
a cormorant entering the night sea.

Last Native

I cross the country along empty roads,
starlings falling like soot from aubergine clouds.
Too early for the burial, I drift back
to the dreams I had the night he died:
hedgehogs balled and stranded after a neap tide.
Badgers aiming sawn-off snouts into bog holes.
Tallboys being pushed against locked doors.

Around the back, his drills are weeded clear.
Cabbage heads squat still as lotuses.
A spade stands sentry against a shed wall.
I drive its seasoned blade into the earth,
work my foot, just as he taught me; see his face
lifting to rain and an ambush of rooks;
the flowers on the hawthorn a frenzied froth.

Kyoto Public Bathhouse

Small, square pools of water, each enough for two
or three on intimate terms: a hot pool,
a bubbling pool, one with ice, and one
electrolysed like a stingray's tank.

Here, we join locals; raised thumbs,
nods, the universal pleasure
of being cleansed – of dust and grime,
of troubling thought, of life's small sorrows.

So that when we emerge into mid-morning,
a blackbird calling across the street
from the lowest branch of a cherry blossom

is a blackbird on a whin bush on the shores
of Lough Dan calling across our youthful heads
to the other end of our lives.

January

The sky flinty, the sea still in its winter strop.
I wait for you by the pier wall, pale towel
under my oxter like a surrendered flag
as I curse the unlearned lessons of 30 years
of late-night, wide-eyed plans. Erratic bursts of spray,
a robin watching from the lea of a rusted hoop.
This plan, yours – a New Year's plunge to mark the all clear.
You arrive in silence, half-smirk, strip off.
If that didn't kill you, this surely will
as in we leap like shaken bottles –
white cells frenzying, coiled worlds unfurling,
new growth bursting through frost,
our screeches skimming across the light
to smash the blown glass of the horizon.

Morning Run

for Deirdre

The usual circuit – house-lined streets, the park,
a stretch of the main road, then back to base.
I go slower than I might – to my mind
at least – so that we can run side by side
and you, as ever, indulge the conceit
that it's you that holds me back
while I fall in with your stride and settle
into mine, words giving way to quickened breath
then rhythm's ease, the steady power of knowing,
each bend and turn, that you are there, your heart
out-beating mine, your pace unflagging,
that when we stop, your hand will touch my back
and I'll root out the key, the door widening
as, together, we step in.

ACKNOWLEDGEMENTS

Acknowledgement and thanks to the editors of the following publications in which a number of the poems in this collection appeared: *Atrium, Crannóg, Cyphers, The Honest Ulsterman, The Irish Times, The Lonely Crowd, Poetry Wales, Prole* and *Southword.* Thanks also to Patrick Cotter of *Southword Editions* for poems previously published in *Earth's Black Chute.*

'Limbo' was anthologised in *Vital Signs: Poems of Illness and Healing* (ed. Martin Dyar, Poetry Ireland, 2022)

A huge thanks to all the poets and writers who have helped me along the way, in particular Vicky Morris, Tom French, Gabriel Fitzmaurice, John McAuliffe, John O'Donnell, Geraldine Mitchell, Jude Nutter, Fergus Cronin, Maurice Devitt, Amanda Bell and all in Hibernian Poets and Poetry Ireland. A special thanks also to Bernard O'Donoghue and Enda Wyley.

Thanks beyond measure to my parents, Nollaig and Vera, and my wonderful siblings Tríona, Diarmaid and Muireann. Deep love and thanks to Deirdre, Luan and Síofra and to Róisín and Dermot.

Love and gratitude to all at the LFC for their camaraderie and support; and to my friends in Goatstown, Glasnevin, Kerry and in the world of law.

And, finally, thanks to Pat Boran for his good humour and astute editorial eye, and to Maria-Simonds Gooding for the use of her powerful work on the front cover.

www.ingramcontent.com/pod-product-compliance
Lightning Source LLC
Chambersburg PA
CBHW030727150426
42813CB00051B/288